Happy Little Dictators Coloring Book

Copyright
Copyright 2019 Offensive Crayons, Inc
All Rights Reserved

International Standard Book Number
ISBN-13: 978-0-578-60708-5

www.offensivecrayons.com

ADOLF HITLER

ELECCIONES

NICOLÁS MADURO

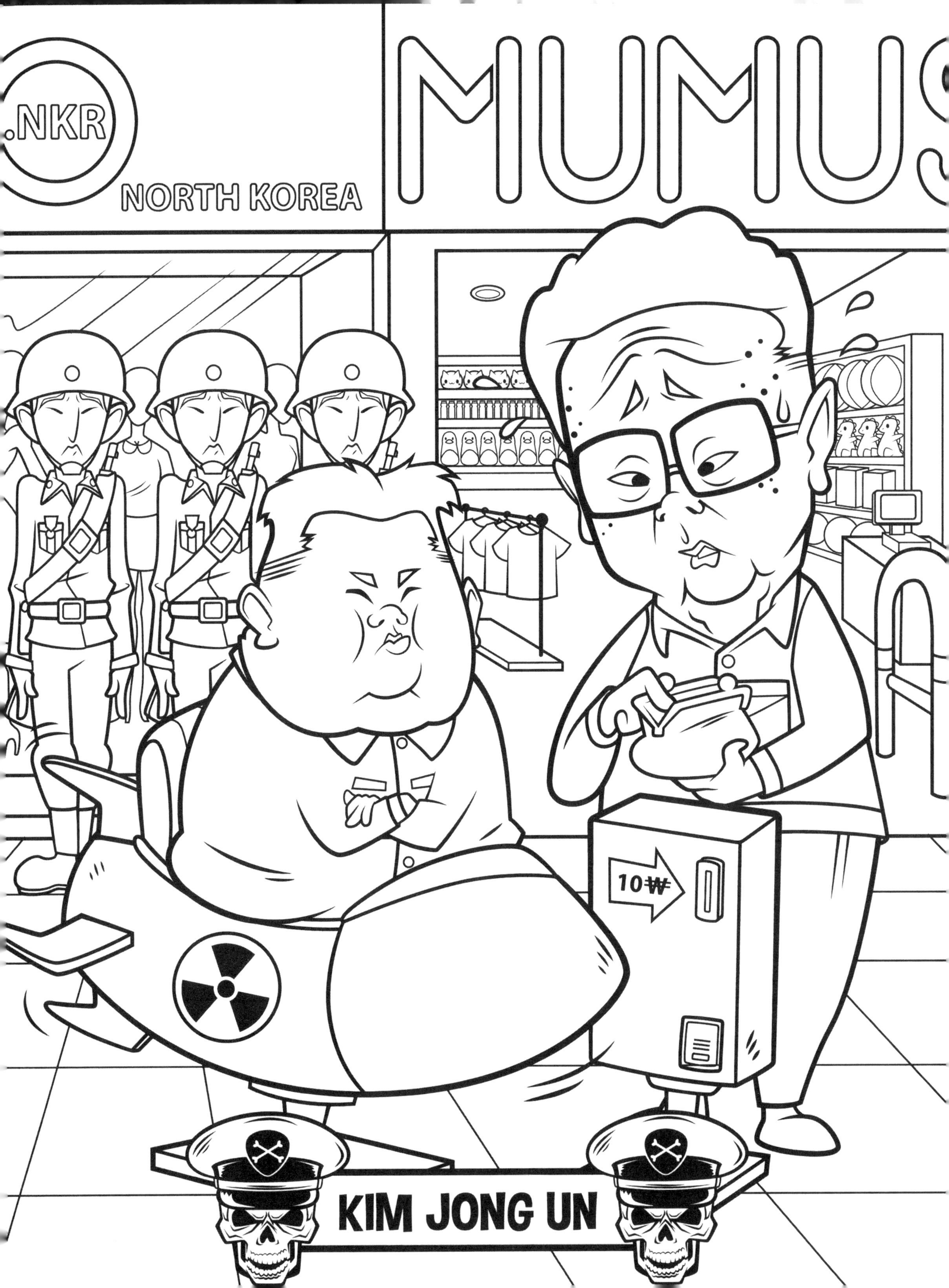
.NKR
NORTH KOREA
MUMUS
10₩
KIM JONG UN

JULIUS CAESAR

JOSEPH STALIN

RODRIGO DUTERTE

MAO ZEDONG

VLADIMIR PUTIN

BENITO MUSSOLINI

SADDAM HUSSEIN

BASHAR AL-ASSAD

FERDINAND MARCOS

FIDEL CASTRO

FRANCISCO FRANCO

GENGHIS KHAN

IDI AMIN

FASHION WEEK

MUAMMAR GADDAFI

NAPOLEON BONAPARTE

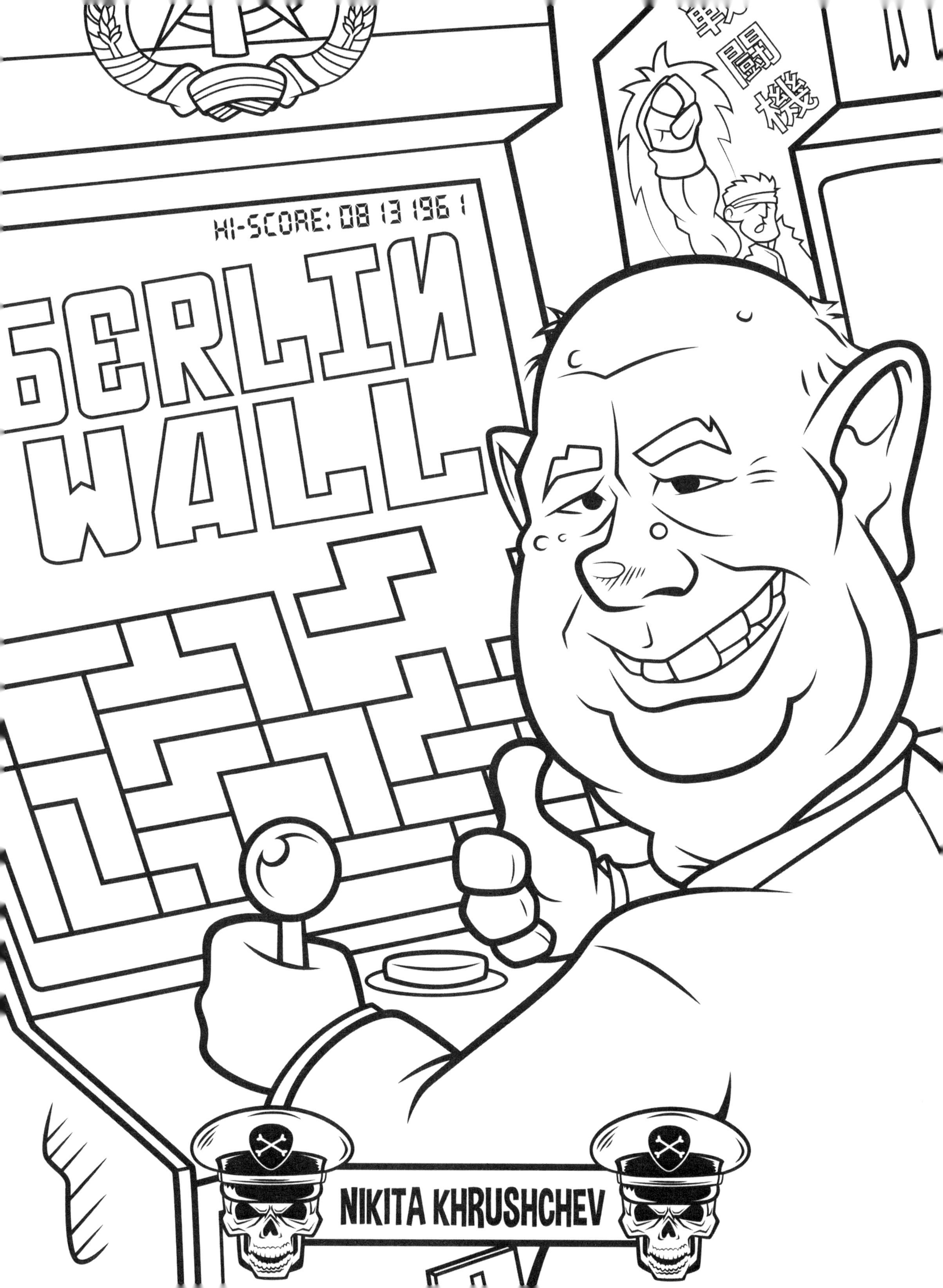
HI-SCORE: 08 13 1961
BERLIN
WALL
NIKITA KHRUSHCHEV

OMAR AL-BASHIR

POL POT

ROBERT MUGABE

TWILIGHT
HARRY POTTER
The Communist Manifesto
50 SHADES OF GRAY
IT

SHINING
IMPERIALISM
Two Tactics of Social Democracy in the Democratic Revolution
the Highest Stage of Capitalism
MEIN CAMP
FIGHT CLUB
LA VIDA INÚTIL DE PITO PÉREZ

VLADIMIR LENIN

ISLAM KARIMOV

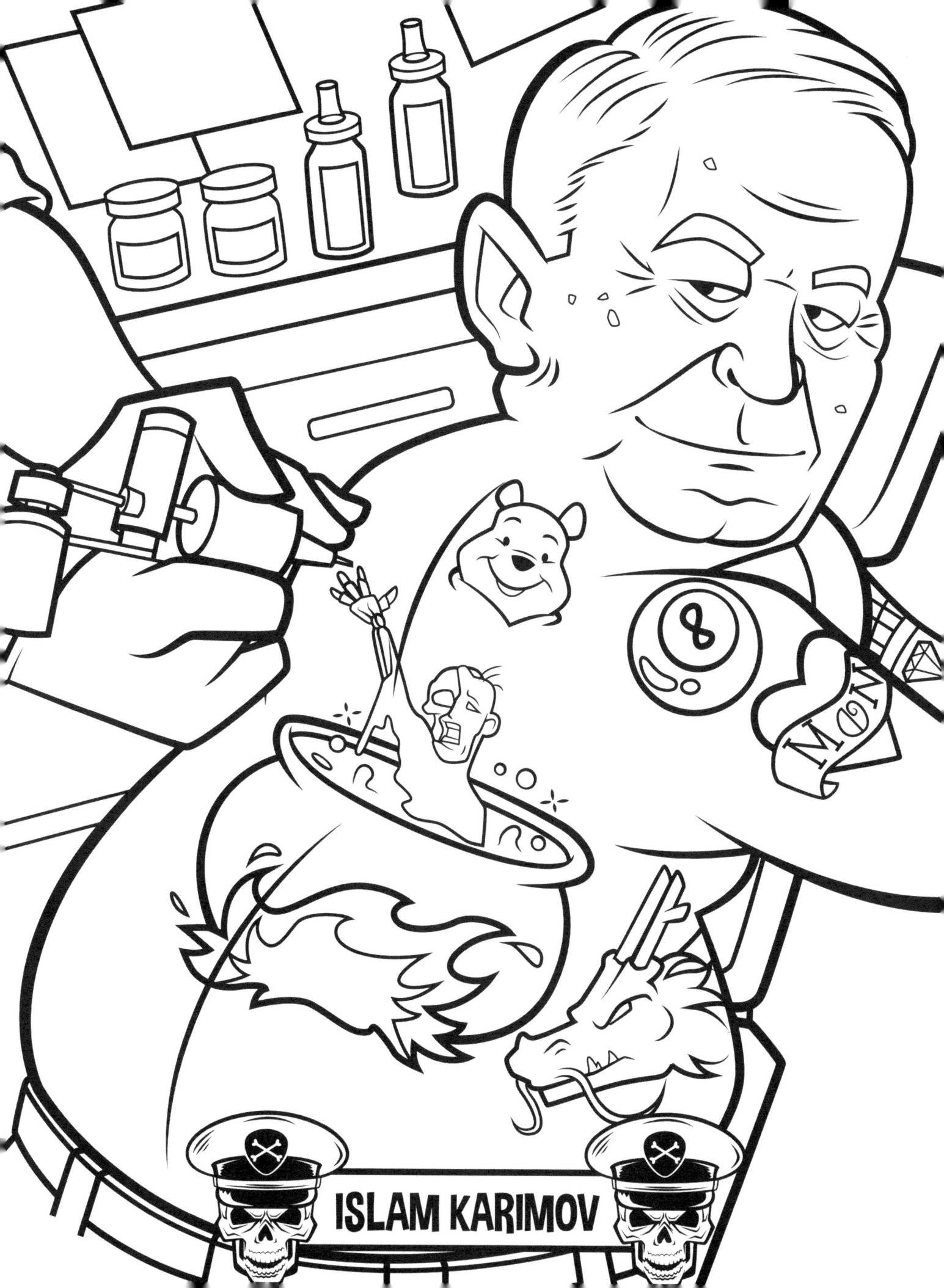

IVAN THE TERRIBLE

NICOLAE CEAUȘESCU

TEODORO OBIANG
NGUEMA MBASOG

RECEP TAYYIP ERDOĞAN

CHIANG KAI-SHEK

ALEXANDER LUKASHENKO